Breaking Ground

B.J. Condrey

Breaking Ground
Copyright: B.J. Condrey
Published: July 2015
Publisher: B.J. Condrey

Unless otherwise noted, all scriptures are from the HOLY BIBLE, NEW INTERNATIONAL VERSION ®. Copyright© 1973, 1978, 1984, 2011 by Biblica, Inc.TM. Used by permission of Zondervan.

Scripture quotations marked (NKJV) are taken from the NEW KING JAMES VERSION®. Copyright© 1982 by Thomas Nelson, Inc. Used by permission. All rights reserved.

Scripture quotations marked (NASB) are taken from the NEW AMERICAN STANDARD UPDATED BIBLE®, copyright©, 1995 by The Lockman Foundation. Used by permission.

Artwork (book cover) by Todd Goodwin of Revibe Media
(www.revibemedia.com)

DEDICATION

Allison my wife, my partner in dreaming, thank you for continuing to encourage and edit everything I write!

Pastor Allen Hickman, who gave me permission to spend over a month of my time in the office writing this book so that Resurrection Life Worship Center could get better at one of the things that Jesus cares most about—*discipling people*. Also, you have taught me above all else that loving Jesus means loving people, *period*.

Billy Martin, you have been a father-figure to me since the day I arrived in Picayune, Mississippi. I can't wait to read *your* book! I love you Billy and thank you for being one of the men in my life that believe in me. You are the real deal and a servant of all. What better can be said of a Christian?

Bro. Dan Finley, PhD, where do I begin? We meet every Wednesday morning from 8-9 so that hopefully, what you have will rub off on me. Your mind is sharp but your spirit is sharper. You see and understand the world of the Spirit more than anybody I know. *I am your disciple*. The world would be better served if you wrote a book rather than I. I hope you will.

Todd Goodwin, you have taught me that if any group of people on the earth should care about excellence, it should be Christians. You are one of the hardest working men I have ever met and the longer I serve beside you, the more I realize that you really do it all to make Jesus look good! I also love our conversations about Jesus, Christianity, and culture. And thank you for making my books look good!

TABLE OF CONTENTS

ABOUT THIS BOOK   i

TIPS BEFORE YOU GET STARTED   iv

KEY: SYMBOLS USED THROUGHOUT BOOK   v

1 THE BEGINNING   2

2 WHAT WENT WRONG?   5

3 WE HAVE A REAL ENEMY   9

4 GOD'S SOLUTION   13

5 BY GRACE, THROUGH FAITH   17

6 A NEW CREATION   22

7 A NEW IDENTITY   26

8 THE SECRET PLACE   30

9 PRAYER   35

10 WORSHIP   38

11 THE WORD   43

12 HEARING GOD   46

13 A LIFE OF TRUST   50

14 A LIFE OF OBEDIENCE   53

15 A LIFE OF REPENTANCE   56

16 WHO IS THE HOLY SPIRIT?   61

17 THE ROLES OF THE HOLY SPIRIT   65

18 THE FRUITS OF THE HOLY SPIRIT   68

19 THE GIFTS OF THE HOLY SPIRIT   72

20 FILLED WITH THE HOLY SPIRIT   76

21 *CHURCH:* THE HOPE OF THE WORLD   81

22 *CHURCH:* BEING A PART   84

23 *CHURCH:* PLAYING YOUR PART   88

24 *CHURCH:* GIVING YOUR PART   91

25 *CHURCH:* THE ONE ANOTHER'S   95

26 EXTRAVAGANT GIVING   100

27 A BIBLICAL WORLDVIEW   104

28 THE HEART OF A SERVANT   108

29 GO! MAKE DISCIPLES   112

30 SHARING YOUR FAITH   116

ABOUT THE AUTHOR   121

RECOMMENDED APPS   123

RECOMMENDED READING   125

ABOUT THIS BOOK

This book is written for new Christians. The purpose is to help you become what the Bible describes as a *disciple* of Christ. Whether you have grown up in church or have never set foot in one, I believe this book will be beneficial. You are not expected to know anything. I am starting from scratch.

What is a disciple? The word 'disciple' comes from the Greek word that means, "to learn." Jesus' original followers were ordinary men and women who followed Him around for three years *learning* about who He was and what He stood for. As they learned, they were then expected to apply what they saw and heard to their own lives. It is no different for us today. If you have accepted Jesus Christ as Savior and Lord, then you too as a child of God are *invited* and *expected* to become more like Him. If you have truly opened your heart to Christ, "discipleship means joy."[1]

Francis Chan wrote, "Somehow many have come to believe that a person can be a 'Christian' without being like Christ. A 'follower' who doesn't follow."[2] There are too many people today in the church who have not truly been impacted and changed by the Jesus who they claim to have accepted. When you said 'yes' to a

---

[1] Dietrich Bonhoeffer, *The Cost of Discipleship* (New York: The Macmillan Company, 1972), 41.
[2] Francis Chan, *Multiply* (Colorado Springs: David C Cook, 2012), 16.

i

relationship with God by accepting Christ His Son, it was only the beginning. Think of this initial decision as stepping over the threshold into the house of faith. Once inside, you are still only in the foyer. The entire house now lies open before you. The journey of discovery and growth has only begun!

To be a disciple of Christ, you need a solid foundation upon which you can build the rest of your life. David wrote, "If the foundations are destroyed, what can the righteous do?"[3] When construction workers erect a building, they work in vain if they build upon a faulty foundation. In time, no matter how nice the finishings, all will crumble. Your walk with Jesus Christ is no different. This book is geared toward helping you acquire a solid, spiritual foundation.

Now, I know that discipleship does not happen by merely reading information in a book. I get that. However, a book like this can play a pivotal role in the process. God once told Hosea, an Old Testament prophet, "My people are destroyed for lack of knowledge."[4] There are certain theological truths as well as habits (what we call *spiritual disciplines)* that you *need* to know.

My prayer is that as you pass through these pages,

> "...the God of our Lord Jesus Christ, the glorious Father, may give you the Spirit of wisdom and

---

[3] Psalms 11:3 NKJV
[4] Hosea 4:6 NKJV

revelation, so that you may know Him better. I pray that the eyes of your heart may be enlightened..."[5]

TIPS BEFORE YOU GET STARTED

Below are a few tips that I believe will maximize your experience over the next six weeks.

- Do not work through this book alone. Find a pastor, a friend, a person, or a couple in your local church to mentor you.

- This book is structured in a 6-week format consisting of 5 modules per week (30 total). You will complete five modules per week and then meet up with your mentor person/couple once per week to discuss.

- Commit fully. You will get out of it what you put into it.

- Do not treat this as classroom material. The goal is transformation, not information. Read with your heart as well as your mind! Start each session by inviting God to reveal Himself to you.

- Mark this book up! Underline, write notes, etc.

- Always work through this book with your Bible and pen beside you. Every day you will be asked to open your Bible and locate certain passages. The main reason I have structured the book in this way is so that at the end of these six weeks, you are able to feed yourself spiritually.

KEY:
SYMBOLS USED THROUGHOUT BOOK

 This symbol means "read."

 This symbol means, "write."

 This symbol means, "prayer." When you see this symbol, a set of remarks will follow intended to coach you in how to pray in response to the material you covered that day. One of the main goals of the book is that you learn how to sit down, all by yourself, and enjoy spending personal time with God. For this reason, each day will end with a time of prayer.

 This symbol means, "Discuss with mentor." When you see this, blank lines will follow. This will conclude each day's lesson. Use this space to write down anything, whether something from that day's reading or something personal, that you would like to discuss when you meet with your mentor. Come up with your own thoughts and questions. As you read that day's lesson, what stirred your heart? What questions do you have? What would you like to discuss further?

WEEK

1

1

THE BEGINNING

Francis Chan writes,

> *"The Bible tells a story. We tend to view the Bible as a bunch of fragmented bits of history, poetry, and moral tales, but in reality, the Bible tells a story. And it's a true story. It's a story that gives meaning to our existence, our daily lives, and to every other story on earth."*[6]

 GENESIS 1:27-2:3

God created the first man, *Adam.* The Bible is clear that human beings did not evolve from some random, accidental, physico-chemical process. An infinite, personal, Holy God chose to create human beings *in his image* by speaking a word. God spoke all things into existence out of nothing.[7] This might seem crazy to you until you consider the alternative—*that matter and energy have existed eternally and that somehow, through an inexplicably precise process, humans somehow arrived on the scene with such things as emotions, hopes, desire for meaningful relationships, a sense of purpose, a moral conscience, and other hardware.* What makes more sense? That relational,

---

[6] Francis Chan, *Multiply* (Colorado Springs: David C Cook, 2012), 139.

[7] What theologians refer to in Latin as *ex nihilo* which means, "out of nothing."

emotional, intelligent, goal-oriented creatures like you and I came from a relational, emotional, intelligent, goal-oriented God, or that we came from lifeless, inorganic matter? God in fact is the more *rational* option. The Christian faith is not *blind* faith.

 GENESIS 2:15-25

After God created Adam, he saw a need to create another gender that could complement him nicely. There are two genders, male and female. He also establishes the institution of marriage between a man and a woman (verse 24). Adam now had someone that he could relate to in a meaningful way.

 PSALMS 8:3-6

Humans are the apex, the climax of all creation. Though Eve was created for Adam, ultimately, Adam and Eve were created for God. Therefore, we occupy a special place in the universe. There is nothing else in existence that possesses the capacity to accept or reject, to love or to hate. We call this *free will*. Even at the risk of you rejecting Him, He gave you *choice* so that love could be a real possibility. So why is the *possibility of love* so important?

 1 JOHN 4:16

_____

_____

_____

_____

The key phrase here is, "God is love." This is God's essential nature. This means that it is impossible for Him to do anything or say anything that is not motivated by love. Never forget this in your journey with the Lord. He loves you. He desires you. He knows how many hairs are on your head.[8] He wanted a very personal, intimate friendship with you before you ever said your first word. Now the risk of giving human beings *free will* should make more sense. He would rather endure the pain of some rejecting Him than create a situation where no one had a real chance to love Him.

God is self-sufficient. He needs nothing. Why would He have gone to the trouble to create humanity except for relationship? He wanted someone to be able to receive, appreciate, and revel in his goodness. Reflect on the goodness of God. Thank God for loving you so much and for pursuing you personally. Open your heart to Him. Tell Him that you want to give Him the love and relationship that He created you to give Him.

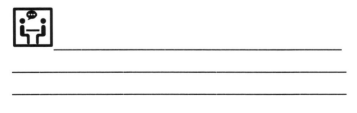

_____

_____
_____
_____

_____

[8] Matthew 10:30

WHAT WENT WRONG?

Over 6 million Jews were killed in the Holocaust.

Fathers and mothers are abandoning children every day because of some drug addiction.

Right now, there is an estimated 4.5 million people in the world trapped in forced sexual exploitation.[9]

Compassion International reports, "Every day, almost 16,000 children die from hunger-related causes. That's one child every five seconds."[10]

Rape. Corporate greed. Murder. Abortion. Suicide. When you look around, it is obvious that something has gone wrong. Really wrong. Horribly wrong. The human heart apart from God is capable of horrendous evil (see Jeremiah 17:9). So what went wrong? *Sin.*

What is sin? It is "anything that is contrary to the law or will of God."[11] Merrill Unger writes, "Sin is everything in

---

[9] "Sex Trafficking in the U.S.," Polaris: Freedom Happens Now, http://www.polarisproject.org/human-trafficking/sex-trafficking-in-the-us (accessed May 21, 2015).

[10] "Hunger Facts," Compassion International, http://www.compassion.com/poverty/hunger.htm (accessed May 21, 2015).

[11] Slick, Matt, "Sin," Christian Apologetics and Research Ministry, https://carm.org/dictionary-sin (accessed May 21, 2015).

the disposition [character] and purpose and conduct of God's moral creatures [that's us] that is contrary to the expressed will of God."[12]

 ROMANS 3:10-18, 3:23

The Bible is clear: *Every human, including you, has sinned.* Each person in some way or another has rebelled against God. *Rebellion* might seem like a strong word, but every sinful thought or word or act goes against God's character and command (given to us in the Bible). **Every sin is selfish at its core**. It is you choosing your way instead of God's way. In the original *Greek* New Testament, one of the words for sin means "to miss the mark." Sin is missing the mark of who God is and all He has commanded.

So where did sin come from?

 GENESIS 2:7-9, 3:1-13

God took great delight in placing Adam and Eve, the first two humans, in a garden brimming with extravagant beauty and life. **He has always wanted only the best for us. His heart has always been good**. So why did God forbid them to eat from the *tree of the knowledge of good and evil* in the middle of the garden? Remember what we discussed on day one about free will. For God to have genuine love humans must have

---

[12] Merrill Unger, R.K. Harrison, Howard F. Vos, and Cyril J. Barber, *The New Unger's Bible Dictionary* (Chicago: Moody Press, 1988), 1198.

choices. He had to allow Adam and Eve the ability to choose against Him. I believe this is the sole reason for God telling the first couple not to eat from this one tree. God, because He is love, gave them an option to reject Him. And they did. In Christianity, this is what is referred to as *The Fall.*

What is the price of sin? What does it cost us?

ISAIAH 59:2

_____

_____

_____

_____

ROMANS 5:12

_____

_____

_____

_____

Sin costs us friendship with God. Being perfect and holy, He cannot overlook sin. It must be dealt with. Through sin, *death* entered the world. Though this includes physical death, the ultimate kind of death that resulted from sin is *spiritual* death. In other words, the human spirit was separated from God because of sin. Sin, in all of its various forms, is the ultimate road block. There is no getting around it. Light and dark cannot have anything to do with each other. For us to have relationship with God, something would have to be done.

Put yourself in God's shoes. You created two humans, surrounded them with indescribable beauty, and offered a perfect loving relationship to them only to see them spit on all of it. Take some time to feel God's pain and to understand His heart so that you have a clear picture of just how ugly sin is. Ask God to place His heart, what He loves and hates, in you.

_____

_____

_____

_____

3

WE HAVE
A REAL ENEMY

Most of us have seen cartoons where a person is trying to make a decision and on one shoulder sits an angel and on the other shoulder, a devil. He is always armed with a pitchfork and offers really bad advice. It is quite silly. The problem with such cartoons is that they blur the line between fantasy and reality. After a while, the idea of Satan himself seems quite silly, and this is when the devil is at his best. He has no problem with people believing that he is not real. This makes it easier for him to work.

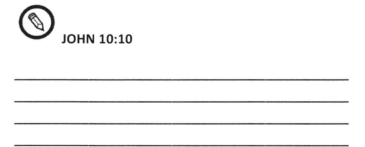 **JOHN 10:10**

_____

_____

_____

_____

Steal. Kill. Destroy. This is extremely aggressive language. Early in human history, there were two brothers, Abel and Cain, the sons of Adam and Eve. One day, each of them brought a separate offering to the

Lord. God approved of Abel's offering but not his brother's. This infuriated Cain.[13] What happened next?

 GENESIS 4:6-7

God, in all of His goodness, was warning Cain. He knew Cain was at a crossroads and was entertaining dark thoughts about murdering his brother. If you keep reading, Cain did not heed God's counsel. He lured Abel out into a field and killed him.

 1 PETER 5:8

A roaring lion. A lion mutilates his prey, tearing it limb from limb, and this is exactly what Satan wants to do with you as well as every other human being. He will use whatever you allow him in his effort to suffocate you. Whether drugs, laziness, bitterness toward someone, emotional brokenness, greed, financial irresponsibility, sexual sins, lust, a poor work ethic, an unhealthy desire for knowledge, insecurity, anxiety, fear, or inattention to your relationship with God, your enemy is lurking quietly behind the curtain waiting to pounce. Do not fool yourself. This is not a game. You get one life from God. One chance. One breath. There are no mulligans.

So where did Satan come from?

 REVELATION 12:3-9 and ISAIAH 14:12-15

---

[13] Genesis 4:5

Satan was once an angel in Heaven. Pride and the desire to stand in God's place and have His worship ultimately destroyed him. He was no longer a worshiper. He wanted the worship. At this moment, God cast him out of Heaven into the pit (Hell). But Satan did not go alone. He had deceived 1/3 of the angels in Heaven and took them with him when he was cast down. The devil and his angels really are *fallen angels.* The battle now rages over man's worship. It is what Satan has wanted all along. And though most people do not become Satan-worshipers, any path that does not have Christ at the center is a path that Satan is quite satisfied with.

 JOHN 8:44

What is the name given for Satan at the end of this verse? _____

What does this tell you? No matter how Satan is going to try to destroy you, his strategy will have something to do with getting you to believe lies. Every victory he wins in a person's life begins subtly with a lie. **Truth is what sets us free,[14] so if truth goes, bondage comes.**

Satan, our arch enemy, will sometimes attack you. His attack could come in the form of physical illness, fear, depression, hopelessness, unbelief, or lies (by no means an exhaustive list). You need to know how to fight back via prayer (waging spiritual warfare). Turn to Romans 16:20 and pray this verse over your life and anybody else that God brings to mind. Another great

---

[14] John 8:32

verse to pray is Matthew 6:13. It is part of the "Lord's Prayer." Satan is aggressive, so you too from time to time must rise up and bind/rebuke Him in the name of Jesus Christ.

_____

_____

_____

_____

4

GOD'S SOLUTION

Adam and Eve sinned in the garden and humans have never stopped since. The Bible teaches that being the guilty party, there is nothing we can do to make things right with God again. **How can dirty hands make something clean again?** It cannot be done according to the Bible. Whether good works, good intentions, or even religious rituals kept ever so diligently, nothing is enough to bridge the gap between a Holy God and sinful man. Only two options remain:

1. The separation between God and humanity will remain infinitely and totally broken. There is no hope for relationship with God. All is lost, a life without God now and an eternity in Hell after death.

2. Or, God Himself, the offended party, takes the initiative and does something that takes care of sin for each person who desires to be reconciled to God.

The good news (what the word *Gospel* actually means) is that God chose option #2! Rather than leave us broken and without hope, He in an act of indescribable mercy set into motion a plan of redemption to repair the connection. What was that plan?

 HEBREWS 10:1-14

In the Old Testament, God chose the nation of Israel to be His own special people. After He set them free from over 400 years of slavery in Egypt, He began showing them who He was and how they were to worship Him. This included a list of how to build a temple, how to arrange everything in the temple, and specific instructions on how to sacrifice animals in just the right way. This is what the passage you just read is speaking of. Now, animal sacrifice probably seems odd due to the fact that in the 21st century, this is not something any of us are doing. But God was doing more than just commanding an odd set of rituals. The blood of the animals served as a precursor to the real thing—*the blood of Jesus Christ that would truly have the power to remove sin once and for all.* The blood of the animals in the Old Testament would cover sin, not remove it. There was nothing magical about the animal blood. Rather, it was to be a constant reminder that God would one day provide His own sacrifice that *would* ultimately eliminate sin.

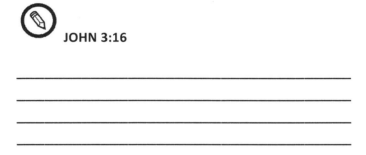 **JOHN 3:16**

_____
_____
_____
_____

Francis Schaeffer writes,

> *"All men are separated from God because of their true moral guilt. God exists, God has a character, God is a Holy God, and when men sin they have true moral guilt before the God who exists. Only the finished, substitutionary work of Christ on the cross*

14

as the Lamb of God—in history, space, and time—is enough to remove this...Christ plus nothing."[15]

 COLOSSIANS 1:19-23

There had to be a perfect sacrifice for sin. Jesus Christ, God's Son, was that sacrifice. Jesus Christ became a human being (the **Incarnation**) and in His early 30's died on a Roman cross for all sin. Christ was the final sacrifice. Three days later, God raised Him from the dead. What is left for you to do?

 ROMANS 10:9, 10:13, and ACTS 2:38

Repent and believe. This is the way to God, to confess that you are a sinner and need Jesus Christ, who died and rose again, to come into your heart and life to forgive you of all of your sins. Jesus saves you (why it is referred to as **salvation** in Christianity). When a person puts their faith in what Christ has done in his or her place, God forgives and welcomes that person back into friendship with Himself. You are probably reading this right now because you have recently *repented* and *believed.*

The Son of God died for you so that God could have a friendship with you. Spend a few moments reflecting upon how valuable you must be in order for Christ to give up all of Heaven to come and die on a

---

[15] Francis Schaeffer, *True Spirituality* (Wheaton: Tyndale House Publishers, 1977), 3.

rugged cross. After doing this, spend a few moments now thinking about how valuable other people must also be because Christ died for them too. Take some time now to pray for three people in your life (family, friends, work) that do not know Jesus. Cry out to God that He would open their eyes like He did yours.

_____

_____

_____

_____

5

BY GRACE,
THROUGH FAITH

Matt Slick writes,

> *"Salvation is the 'saving' of a sinner from the righteous judgment of God. When someone appeals to God and seeks forgiveness in Jesus, his sins are forgiven. He is cleansed. His relationship with God is restored...Salvation is a free gift."*[16]

ROMANS 6:23

_____

_____

_____

_____

EPHESIANS 2:8-9

The beauty and uniqueness of Christianity is that it is the only major religion that is fundamentally about what God has done for you rather than what you can do

---

[16] Slick, Matt, "Salvation," Christian Apologetics and Research Ministry, https://carm.org/dictionary-salvation (accessed May 29, 2015).

for God. The Bible is clear—*you cannot earn your salvation.* You are too sinful, too depraved, too dark, and too offensive. The verse you previously wrote clearly states that salvation is a *gift* from God. You could never deserve it. In fact, justice demands that you are punished for sin. But Jesus Christ, being perfect, took your place on the cross and with His death, paid the penalty for your sins, so that all you have to do now is come humbly to Him with a childlike heart and trust in Him that His sacrificial death is sufficient for God to forgive all of your sins. He accomplished it. He has done it. The formula for salvation is *Christ plus nothing.* You cannot add good works or good character or good intentions. Isaiah wrote that your very best effort is nothing more than filthy rags before God. We are that sinful and He is that Holy.

So, *by grace* simply means that the salvation offered to you is a gift. A gift is something you do not work for or earn. You either receive it or you don't. You cannot run out the door and go put in a few hours of work to pay for it. If someone gave you a gift on Christmas morning and you started making promise after promise that as soon as the holidays were over, you were going to pick up an extra shift to pay that person back, the individual would look at you like you were crazy. Why? You do not work for a gift. The only choice to be made is whether or not you will receive it or reject it.

While *by grace* has to do with the nature of salvation, the second part of the phrase—*through faith*—addresses how it can be acquired. *Faith* means that you choose personally to *trust* in the finished work of Christ on the cross to be made right with God. The "through faith" part of the equation means that though Christ has done all that needs to be done for you to be saved, you still have to make the personal decision to believe in Him and trust (i.e. faith) in what He has accomplished on your behalf. *Faith* is your personal response to the grace that has been made available. Think of it as sitting down on Christmas morning and simply receiving the gift.

 ROMANS 3:21-26

God offered you salvation in His Son (grace). You chose to believe in Him (faith). What does God do next? *Justify you.* **Justification** in Christian thought is the "legal act of God" in which He declares you forgiven, no longer guilty of sin, and positively righteous, clothed with the perfection of Christ himself.[17] Now, clothed in Christ's righteousness, you can approach God and begin living your life in Him, through Him, with Him, and for Him!

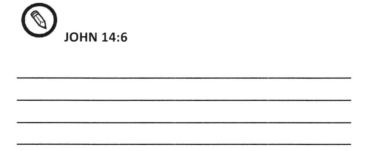 **JOHN 14:6**

_____

_____

_____

_____

---

[17] Wayne Grudem, *Systematic Theology: An Introduction to Biblical Doctrine* (Grand Rapids: Zondervan, 1994), Kindle e-book.

ACTS 4:12

_____

_____

_____

_____

His love for you and acceptance of you is based on Christ, *not* your performance? Whether it has been your worst day or best day, you can enjoy God's presence. Reflect on how wonderful and freeing this truth is and in prayer, thank Him for it. Also, pray for other Christians in your life right now one-by-one that might not understand this pivotal truth. Include your pastor in this list. Pray for God to remind him that God is for him, not against him.

_____

_____

_____

_____

WEEK

A NEW CREATION

---

 2 CORINTHIANS 5:14-21

Jesus once told a Pharisee by the name of Nicodemus, "Unless one is born again, he cannot see the kingdom of God."[18] When you opened your heart to Jesus Christ as Savior and Lord, He came, *in the person of the Holy Spirit*, to live inside you (more on this in week 4). You are now the *temple* of the Holy Spirit (as opposed to a tent or building structure like in the Old Testament). When He enters a person, He makes that person brand new!

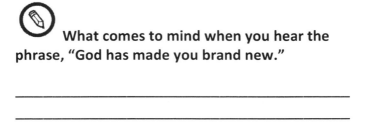 **What comes to mind when you hear the phrase, "God has made you brand new."**

_____

_____

_____

 1 THESSALONIANS 5:23

Every human is made up of three parts—*spirit, soul, and body.* Your body is the physical casing, the shell, for

---

[18] John 3:3 NKJV

everything else. Your soul is the seat for your intellect, personality, emotions, and imagination. And your spirit? When Adam and Eve committed that first sin, our spirit died. This is part of what Paul meant when he wrote, "Therefore, just as sin entered the world through one man, and death through sin, and in this way death came to all people, because all sinned."[19] As mentioned last week, the *death* that Paul is referring to includes a spiritual death, that is, a *separation* from God. Because you and I are born into sin (Psalms 51:5), even at birth your spirit is dead to God.

 1 CORINTHIANS 6:17

At salvation, the Holy Spirit entered you and joined with your spirit. Marriage is a perfect symbol. The Bible says that when two people are married, the *two* become *one.* The Holy Spirit has joined with what was your *dead-to-God* spirit and has now made you alive to Him. This is what Paul is referring to when he wrote, "And you *He made alive*, who were dead in trespasses and sins."[20] Ultimately, Jesus Christ died on a cross to bring *dead* people to life. Life? John, one of Jesus' disciples, wrote, "And this is eternal life, that they may know You, the only true God, and Jesus Christ whom You have sent."[21]

Hundreds of years before Jesus' earthly life and ministry, there was an Old Testament prophet named

---

[19] Romans 5:12
[20] Ephesians 2:1 NKJV
[21] John 17:3 NKJV

Ezekiel. Looking ahead, God told this prophet of what He would eventually accomplish.

EZEKIEL 36:26

_____

_____

_____

_____

_____

When a person comes to Christ, he or she undergoes a _metamorphosis_. Normally, this word refers to the process a caterpillar goes through on its way to becoming a butterfly. A butterfly is beautiful, graceful, and possesses an unlimited freedom compared to what it possessed in its previous state. The caterpillar did not simply change colors or gain wings. You do not look at a butterfly and think to yourself, "Wow, that caterpillar has really improved." No! Instead, when you look at a butterfly, you probably do not even remember that what you are looking at was once a slow, round, lethargic creature. A radical transformation has occurred. This living "thing" has completely changed. It is fundamentally different.

This is what has happened to you! Christ has made you new, complete with a brand new heart.

Pray for a deeper revelation that you are in fact _new_! As you pray, let faith arise. This _newness_ means that in your life, all sin can be overcome and all pain healed. Ask God to show you over the next few days, weeks, and months just how "new" you really are. Now, pray for other Christians that you know that need to be reminded of this truth.

_____

_____

_____

_____

7

A NEW IDENTITY

A popular phrase that is frequently tossed around in our pluralistic society is, "We are all God's children." In other words, no matter what you believe or do not believe, you are God's child. This phrase is nice, tolerant, and quite comforting. The *problem* is that the Bible does not teach this.

 JOHN 1:1-13

The "Word" in the first few verses is referring to Jesus Christ. Though you just read verse 12, take a moment to write it out.

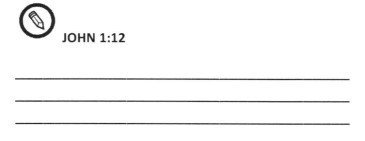 **JOHN 1:12**

_____

_____

_____

_____

Theologically (the study of God), this is one of the more important verses in the entire Bible. Only when a person receives Christ is he or she brought into the family of God. **We are all God's creation, but not all His children.** A person must make an intentional decision to receive Christ to be declared God's *son* or *daughter.*

GALATIANS 3:26, 4:4-7, and ROMANS 8:14-17

At salvation, you received the Holy Spirit. Only Christians have the Holy Spirit, and these verses tell us that the Spirit is inside of every Christian whispering, "God is your Daddy."

MATTHEW 6:9

_____

_____

_____

_____

Tomorrow you will read more of this passage. For now, I want you to focus on this verse. Jesus is beginning to teach his disciples about prayer (how to listen and talk to God). The very first instruction He gives is for His followers (then and now) to address God as _Daddy_ when praying. This is very intimate and personal. Jesus could have told us to start our prayers by addressing God as _Master_, _King_ of Kings, _Lord_, _Creator_, _All-Powerful One_, _All-Knowing One_, _Glorious God_, or _Majesty_ (to only name a few). But He didn't. Instead, He looked into the eyes of people like us and said, "When you pray, think of God as your perfectly good Dad. Do not be afraid of Him. Be yourself and open your heart in a very real way. Interact with Him as any child would who is absolutely confident of their father's love, acceptance, and approval."

Let these truths sink into your spirit and heart:

27

- Because of Christ in you, God is your Dad.
- Because of Christ in you, God loves you passionately and wants the best for you.
- Because of Christ in you, God totally accepts you.
- Because of Christ in you, God takes immense pleasure in calling you His child.
- Because of Christ in you, God loves you as His child on your worst, most sinful day just as much as He does on the day you feel like you got everything right.

This is not a religion of formulas or rituals. God is not looking for people to do a few household chores. Rather, He has reclaimed you through the blood of Jesus Christ in order to enjoy relationship with you! It is always, first and foremost, about the *heart*. You are God's child. He is your Dad. How can you live with insecurity any longer? Christians ought to be the most humble, confident people on the earth. Your identity now at the deepest level can be stated in three words: *child of God.*

 Take some time to think about what it really means to have God as your Dad every single minute of every single day. Personally invite Him to be your Dad in *every* area of your life. Ask Him for greater revelation. After you ask Him, sit still for a few minutes. Let Him love on you, affirm you, and show you His heart. He might speak to you through a thought or feeling.

8

THE SECRET PLACE

Imagine a man and woman who although married, never spent alone time together. They go out to eat in groups, hang out with other couples, go to church together, and workout at the same gym side-by-side. So far, so good, right? But what if refused to be alone together? Look at what they would be missing out on:

- No meals in the privacy of their own home where they are able to eat slowly, catch up on their day, and forget about the world.
- No early evening walks.
- No meaningful conversations from the heart.
- No intimacy.
- No sex (not the same thing as intimacy).

The couple would practically become roommates, nothing more, and in time, would probably go their separate ways. Sadly, many Christians interact in such a way with the infinitely-personal, loving God. It is not much of a relationship. It is definitely not what Jesus Christ had in mind when he gave Himself to be torn, mutilated, and hung on a cross. He died to have a deeply personal, passionate friendship with you.

 MATTHEW 5:1-2 and 6:5-15

Jesus was sitting on a mountain teaching his disciples (and others within earshot) about prayer. One of the first instructions He gave was, "When you pray, go into your room, close the door and pray to your Father, who is unseen."[22] Jesus expects *every* follower to spend personal, private time with Him on a consistent, regular basis. This is time that you set aside, block out all other distractions, and converse with Him. This time can include everything from reading your Bible, singing worship songs, journaling, praying over issues in your own life, praying for others, or sitting still to see if He might speak to you by dropping a thought into your head/heart. Quite often, your time with Jesus will involve several of these activities, and before you know it, your time with God will begin to take shape.

Jesus is communicating that you need to spend time with God daily where you have intentionally set aside all distractions (including technology) in order to connect with God in a simple, meaningful way.

PSALMS 46:10

The busier life gets, the more you have to schedule in that which is most important. Your personal time with God is no different. I believe this is part of what Jesus was saying when He said to go into your room and shut the door. Have a set time and place that you have designated for God. For me, I get up before work, make my coffee, pull up the blinds, and sit in the same chair by a particular window every morning. Now, sometimes I like to shake things up and go for a walk to connect with God. But 95% of the time, I sit in that same chair at about the same time every morning. It is scheduled. It is not up for debate. I have intentionally developed this

---

[22] Matthew 6:6

habit in my life as a way to make sure, no matter what is going on, that my friendship with God remains a top priority and continues to grow. The best things in life usually do not come by accident.

Another advantage of having a set place and time is that when you go to that *secret place*, your spirit and soul become trained over time to submit. Your mind no longer screams at you for slowing down, pushing everything to the side, and focusing on God. You're "inside" recognizes what time it is because of your "outside" routine (internal/external). This is time for God, *period.*

Take a few moments and come up with a few possibilities for the following two questions:

1. What are some potential places that might be an option for you to designate as *that* secret place for you and God?

    _____

    _____

    _____

2. What are some potential times during the day that might be an option for you to designate as your set time with God?

    _____

    _____

    _____

Over the course of the next couple of weeks, experiment with different places and times you wrote down. Then, make your decision. Commit! And remember, some days you will have to be flexible. Life happens. However, it is still best to have that set place and time. You can never be too intentional with something as important as your relationship with God.

JEREMIAH 9:23-24

_____

_____

_____

_____

_____

_____

This is how much God longs for relationship with you. There is no pressure to get a formula right. The main thing is for you to find your place, set your time, and open your heart to Him regularly. He can take it from there!

Talk to the Lord about the kind of relationship you desire with Him. Be affectionate. Ask Him what He has in mind. After doing so for a few minutes, pray for the people in your life that you believe are more _religious_ than _relational_ in their faith. Pray that God would break through their cold religion and call them into a loving, dynamic friendship.

_____

9

PRAYER

Prayer is conversation with God. There are times you talk and there are times you listen. For most people, the talking comes easily. The listening part must be cultivated over time.

 LUKE 11:1-13

In the passage you just read, a few men were hungry to know how to pray, so they asked Jesus to teach them. What does He do? He teaches them. They were spiritually hungry, something God both loves and rewards. Jesus then launches into what is famously labeled, *The Lord's Prayer.* Yesterday you read Matthew's version. The prayer starts with, "Our Father in heaven, hallowed be Your name." The word "hallow" means "to honor as holy."[23] In other words, when you sit down in your secret place to spend time with God in prayer, do not begin with a list of requests. Instead, start by worshipping Him. **God is not a vending machine.** Always take a few moments to look at Him, worship Him. Praise Him, thank Him, and delight in Him. Then, after you have done this for a while, move on to whatever questions or requests are in your heart that day. One of the great advantages of beginning prayer

---

[23] "Hallow," Dictionary.com, http://dictionary.reference.com/browse/hallow (accessed June 4, 2015).

with worship is that it helps you make sure your time with God is actually about God and not just about you. Even prayer can become selfish.

There are different kinds of prayer and they are appropriate in different moments. I found the following description on a Jesuit website to be helpful:

> "Sometimes we bless or adore God (**prayer of blessing and adoration**). Other times we ask God for something for ourselves (**prayer of petition**). Sometimes we pray for others (**prayer of intercession**). We also thank God in prayer (**prayer of thanksgiving**). Finally, we can also praise God (**prayer of praise**). We can pray silently or aloud. We can pray alone or with others. Praying with others is called **communal prayer**."[24]

Paul commands all Christians to "pray without ceasing."[25] So, while praying is something you definitely do in your personal time with God, it is also something you can do in your heart, under your breath, all throughout the day. Let prayers rise from your heart continually. Be a person of prayer.

 PSALMS 62:8

_____

_____

---

[24] "Prayer and Forms of Prayer," Loyola Press. A Jesuit Ministry, http://www.loyolapress.com/prayer-and-forms-of-prayer.htm (accessed June 4, 2015).
[25] 1 Thessalonians 5:17 NKJV

Remember, prayer is not complicated. Anytime you talk with a friend, you are not worried about saying something the right or wrong way. You are just yourself. You share what is on your heart. A true friend is someone that you do not have to perform for, nor do you have to pretend to be someone you are not.

 JOHN 15:15

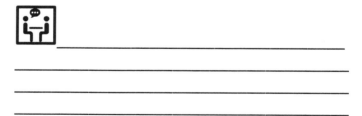 David wrote, "I am a man of prayer."[26] Pray the prayer of the disciples: "Lord, teach [me] to pray." If you are afraid that you will not be good at it, tell Him. Be honest. What do you believe God wants your prayer life to look like? Pour out your heart to Him right now and let Him know just how much you desire an intimate, powerful life of prayer.

---

[26] Psalms 109:4

10

WORSHIP

Every human being, without exception, worships someone or something.

Corrie Tin Boom, a Dutch citizen who helped save over 800 Jews during the Holocaust before being discovered and imprisoned,[27] used to say that in every human heart sits a throne and a cross. Following Christ means that at some point in your past, you chose to step down off the throne, invited Jesus to sit in His rightful place, and then climbed upon the cross.

GALATIANS 2:20-21

---

[27] "Corrie ten Boom," bio., http://www.biography.com/people/corrie-ten-boom-21358155 (accessed June 8, 2015).

Though worship includes singing songs of thanksgiving, adoration, and praise to God, it is so much more. Ultimately, worship is a life lived both *to* and *for* God. Remember day six? You are now a *new* creation, called to live a life centered around Christ, *not* yourself.

As stated, though worship ultimately is about living your entire life unto God, one of the best ways to worship God is with your words and with music.

 PSALMS 29:2 and PSALMS 150 *(entire chapter)*

In the New King James Version of the Bible, the word "worship" occurs 197 times, the word "praise" 277 times, and the word "thank" (in all of its forms such as *thanksgiving*) 139 times. One of the best things you can do is to play an instrument or play a few songs and sing them aloud to God. During these times of worship with song, you are ultimately declaring to Him how great He is and how much He means to you. Music is one of the best ways to pour our affection out on Him. Whether sitting alone by a window or in a group of people (a small group, a church, etc.), singing to God is beautiful and something He treasures. This in part is what the phrase "ministering to God" meant in Old Testament times. As crazy as it is, the God of the Universe allows Himself to be ministered to by His people.

When you take time to worship God through song whether in private or public, Christ is exalted in your thoughts and in your heart. When this happens, you become better suited to now worship God in every area of your life.

- *Worship is* obeying God in the smallest details.
- *Worship is* thanking God when you feel like complaining.
- *Worship is* refusing to gossip when it would be easy to do so.
- *Worship is* sacrificing something for someone else though it hurts to do so.
- *Worship is* sitting still in a quiet place, opening your Bible and heart, and seeking God through its pages.
- *Worship is* whispering to God all day under your breath, "I love you. I love you."
- *Worship is* being a part of a local church and serving people.
- *Worship is* repenting when He convicts you of sin.
- *Worship is* forgiving someone because God forgave you when you did not deserve it.
- *Worship is* prioritizing your family above work, hobbies, or friends.
- *Worship is* sharing your faith with someone who does not know Christ.
- *Worship is* sitting still staring at a sunrise and thinking about how wonderful God must be to create such beauty.
- *Worship is* creating a piece of art to honor God (this does not mean that the piece of art is overtly religious).
- *Worship is* giving your employer (whether you like the job or not) 100%.

Delesslyn A. Kennebrew writes,

> *"Worship is not the slow song that the choir sings. Worship is not the amount you place in the offering basket. Worship is not volunteering in children's church. Yes, these may be acts or expressions of worship, but they do not define what true worship really is. True worship, in other words, is defined by*

40

the priority we place on who *God is in our lives and where God is on our list of priorities. True worship is a matter of the heart expressed through a lifestyle of holiness."*[28]

You get the idea. **All things are spiritual.** Every activity under the sun can be performed as an act of worship if you make it so. Be a worshipper!

Pray to God to give you a heart of worship. Play a worship song right now and sing it to God. As you do, He may talk to you. He may share a burden that is on His heart. Or, at the end of the song, He may lead you to pray that the Holy Spirit would give other Christians you know a heart of worship. You can also pray that God would release a *spirit of worship* in your local church family. Sing your heart out and see where He leads you in prayer.

_____

_____
_____
_____

---

[28] Kennebrew, Delesslyn, "What Is True Worship?," Christianity Today, http://www.christianitytoday.com/biblestudies/bible-answers/spirituallife/what-is-true-worship.html (accessed June 8, 2015).

41

WEEK

11

THE WORD

The Bible is sometimes referred to as *The Word*, *God's Word*, *The Word of God,* and/or *The Scriptures.*

What is written in the Bible is God's self-revealing letter to all people, especially Christians. Once spoken by a real God to real people, it was then recorded and passed down. The Holy Spirit oversaw this entire process in order to assure that the text is without error (inerrant) and a perfectly accurate description of God as well as all matters of faith. In a nutshell, the Bible tells us what is real.

 2 TIMOTHY 3:16-17

The Holy Spirit inspired each word. The 19th century Danish philosopher Soren Kierkegaard wrote, "When you read God's Word, you must constantly be saying to yourself, 'It is talking to me, and about me.'" It is to be read, taken seriously, meditated upon, believed, internalized, and lived. If you do, God promises that as a result of sowing God's Word into your heart, you will be "complete, thoroughly equipped for every good work."

God's wants you, as one of His children, to experience great pleasure and joy when reading His Word. In the following passage, pay attention to the promise God gives you if you choose to make His Word a meaningful part of your daily life.

PSALMS 1:1-3

God wants to show you which way to go in your life from one decision to the next. This next verse would be a great verse for you to memorize!

 PSALMS 119:105

_____

_____

_____

God also wants to strengthen you through the Scriptures when you are struggling.

 PSALMS 119: 25, 28

When Jesus lived upon the Earth, He had access to the Old Testament. It was His Bible (the New Testament was not written until after His death and resurrection) and He knew it well.

 MATTHEW 4:1-11

Each time that Satan tempted Jesus in an effort to get Him to sin, Jesus resisted sin by declaring a verse from the Old Testament. God's Word, both written and spoken, contains His power. Jesus knew this. Paul writes that God's Word is the "sword of the Spirit,"[29] the only *offensive* weapon mentioned regarding the spiritual armor. God tells each Christian to put this armor on at the beginning of each day.

The bottom line is this: *There is power in God's Word to minister to you, empower you, help you, convict you, show you who God is, guide you, and to do whatever else God is wanting to accomplish in and through your life.*

 HEBREWS 4:12

Practice meditating. This can be a type of prayer. It is a spiritual discipline that saints have benefitted greatly from all throughout history. Pick a verse that you either read or wrote today. Block out all other thoughts. Do not ask God for anything. Sit still for five minutes looking at whatever verse you have chosen in a prayerful, thoughtful manner. Pick it apart. See if the Holy Spirit gives insight into God's heart or your personal life as you meditate.

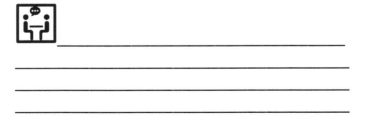

---

[29] Ephesians 6:17

12

HEARING GOD

Pastor Allen Hickman always says, "It is the right of every Christian to hear God's voice." Because of the substitutionary sacrifice of Jesus Christ, God does not hold your sin against you. He removed your sin and guilt so that you could know God and become like Him.

Fundamental to knowing God is being able to hear Him speak. After all, how in the world would you get to know someone without any means of communication?

JOHN 10:27-28

_____

_____

_____

_____

_____

_____

Every Christian is a child of God. What _good_ dad does not long in his heart to interact with his child in an ongoing, meaningful way?

ACTS 13:1-3

You just read about a group of people wholeheartedly seeking God through prayer and fasting. What happened? God, the Holy Spirit, spoke. That simple! In this particular story, He told them what to do next. God is a speaking God! It is His delight to speak into the heart of every person who wants to hear what He has to say. Below are some ways that God speaks:

- **Thoughts**: A thought will pop into your mind that at first seems to come from nowhere. Then, after a few hours or even days, you realize that you cannot get that thought out of your head. Quite often this is God's Spirit speaking to you.
- **Bible**: You will be reading the Bible when suddenly, a word or phrase or even entire verse "jumps" off the page. This is a good time to stop and see what God is saying.[30]
- **Movies**: Whether a statement by one of the characters or something that occurs during the movie, God can use it to speak to you.
- **Music**: I am not necessarily referring to "Christian" music. There may be a line in a song that really gets your attention. In some instances, God might be trying to say something to you.
- **Books**: Once again, I am not necessarily referring to "Christian" literature. Whether fiction or nonfiction, the Lord can speak to you through the text.

---

[30] In my book, *The Word As A Vehicle* (available on Amazon), I call this the "Highlighter Effect." This book is available in both kindle and paper format on Amazon.

- **Conversations**: Someone says something that later, God brings to mind and seems to emphasize.
- **Preaching:** During a sermon, something is said that seems to really pierce your heart.
- **Nature**: God uses something in nature to speak to you.
- _____: This empty blank represents ALL of the other ways that God can speak to us. Do not limit Him. He is creative and will quite often interact with you in a very unique, individually crafted manner. He is an intimate God.

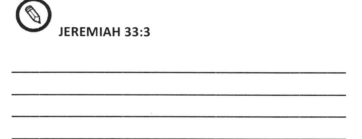

JEREMIAH 33:3

_____

_____

_____

_____

It is very important that you keep in mind that hearing God's voice is something you get better at over time. Every person, especially in the beginning, struggles with whether or not a thought is "God speaking" or "just a random thought." Over time and especially as you spend more and more time in God's Word, you will learn to distinguish God's voice from all other voices. I believe it is a process He enjoys, so do not get stressed. Enjoy the journey. Any relationship is a process. And remember, *God does not mind repeating Himself.* For this I am so thankful! He is patient. You are in God's field, His garden, and He is the *gardener.*[31] Stay planted in Him and the rest will begin "falling" into place.

Right now, memorize John 10:27 one phrase at a time. As you do, pray each phrase to God. Put your own words to it. Invite the Lord to speak to you. Make it clear to Him that you want His voice to be at the center of your life. Be the son/daughter that refuses to settle for a voiceless faith. Daddy loves to talk to His children. Throw out the red carpet and wait for Him.

_____

_____

_____

_____

---

[31] John 15:1

13

A LIFE OF TRUST

If you do not trust someone, you will not let them babysit your kids. If you do not trust someone, you will not invite them to your home. If you do not trust someone, you will not share intimate details from your life with that individual. *Trust* is paramount, an essential ingredient in the formation and growth of any relationship.

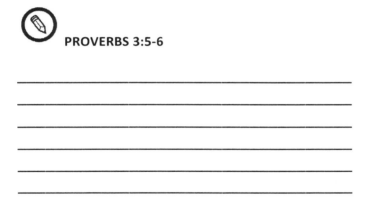

PROVERBS 3:5-6

_____

_____

_____

_____

_____

_____

When you became a Christian, you had to place your trust in the substitutionary sacrifice of Jesus in order to be forgiven, justified, and declared right before God. How silly would it be to start this spiritual journey by trusting in Christ to forgive you, but then not trust Christ to lead, guide, help, and perfect you afterwards?

In order to truly trust God with all of your heart, you must be convinced who He is. The following verse provides further reason why you can trust Him with all of your heart.

 1 PETER 5:7

In one of the first teachings of Jesus, He invited people into a life of trust free from all *anxiety* and *fear*. How is this possible? By keeping our eyes fixed on the caring, loving, provisional nature of Daddy God. John, one of Jesus' original 12 disciples, wrote "There is no fear in love. But perfect love drives out fear..."[32] If you will allow God's love to have its way in your heart, *trusting* Him will be an automatic by-product. It will not be difficult.

 MATTHEW 6:25-34

 Trust in God is rooted in *knowing* God. You cannot trust someone you do not know. Is there an area in particular (or maybe more than one) where you are having a difficult time trusting Him? Why do you think that is? This would be a great time to open your heart in a vulnerable way and have an honest conversation with God. He is your Dad, a perfect Dad.

_____

---

[32] 1 John 4:18

14

A LIFE OF OBEDIENCE

Obedience?

What an unpopular word in our free-spirited, individualistic society! However, obedience is very, very important to God.

In arranging the order of topics in this book, I made sure that yesterday's topic, *a life of trust,* preceded today's topic, *obedience*. The reason is simple. Both go hand-in-hand. You cannot obey God from the heart if you do not trust Him first. Think about it. If you do not really believe that He wants the best for you (according to what is in His heart), then you will be too suspicious of Him to obey. A *trusting heart* is the womb from which *obedience* is birthed.

JOHN 14:15, 21

_____

_____

_____

_____

_____

_____

_____

It is not that you need to obey to *prove* your love to God. This is not at all what Jesus was teaching. Rather, obedience is an expression of your love for Him.

If you are not willing to do what He says, then you must not care about pleasing Him, and if you do not care much about pleasing Him, how could you say you love Him?

As a new creature, the cry of your heart should now be, "*Your* kingdom come, *Your* will be done."[33] May your heart long to thrill Him through childlike obedience. In all areas, God is willing to instruct you in the way you should go.[34] Is this not what a good dad does? Your job is, similar to that of a child, not to analyze His command. Did He speak? Then that is enough. Do what he said. The results are always up to Him, not you.

 ACTS 9:1-22

God told Ananias to do something that defied all reason and common sense. Saul (before he became Paul) had been dragging Christ-followers to jail and even killing some of them. Then, God reveals Himself to Saul on the road to Damascus. However, based on my interpretation of this passage, Ananias did not know this. All he knew was that God wanted him to go pray for a man who was looking for people just like himself in order to hurt or kill. This, from a rational perspective, made absolutely no sense. As a matter of fact, these instructions appeared totally foolish. If Ananias would

---

[33] Matthew 6:9
[34] Psalms 32:8 NKJV

have weighed the pros and cons or tried to decide whether or not to obey based on *reason,* he would not have obeyed. God require great trust of Ananias that day.

There are times that He is going to command you to do something that will not make immediate sense. He may tell you to buy someone's meal, give away a vehicle, end a relationship, witness to a co-worker, serve in the Children's Ministry at your local church, start reading your Bible, pursue a dream He has put in your heart, take an orphan fishing, or mow a widow's yard. Who knows! That is part of the adventure and what keeps faith exciting.

Take some time today to ask God for an obedience heart. This is a dangerous prayer! You must mean it. Pray that God would instill deep in your spirit an understanding of the importance of obedience. Ask the Holy Spirit to show you where you are being obedient. Feel His pleasure. Now pray for the Holy Spirit to show you where you are currently disobedient. He loves you so do not be afraid of correction. If He shows you an area you are not obeying, tell Him you are sorry and ask Him immediately for the strength to obey.

_____
_____
_____
_____

15

A LIFE OF REPENTANCE

 PSALMS 51:1-13

This Psalm was written by David, the greatest king Israel had ever known. He was a man after God's heart. However, he was also a man who committed many, many sins. In the passage you just read, David is pouring out his heart in repentance to God. He is telling God how deeply sorry he is for committing adultery and then arranging a murder to cover it.

Sin is any thought, word, attitude, or action that goes against the character and will of God. Paul wrote, "Be imitators of God as dear children."[35] Because God desires above all else for you to know Him and become like Him, He deals with the sin in your heart and life.

Repentance as a Christian involves three things:

1. Being sorrowful in your heart that you have sinned against the God who loves you.
2. Telling God that you are sorry.
3. Turning away from that sin and turning toward God (which will involve a lifestyle change in that area).

---

[35] Ephesians 5:1 NKJV

 **ROMANS 2:4**

_____

_____

_____

_____

It is so important to remember that when God convicts us, He is actually showing His kindness and goodness.

 HEBREWS 12:4-11

When He disciplines you, He is treating you as a son/daughter. If you did not belong to Him, He would not bother. As a dad, I would never walk up to a daughter of a complete stranger and discipline her. For what reason then (according to this passage) does God discipline you? _Holiness._ He wants you to look exactly like His Son.

 2 CORINTHIANS 7:8-10

Conviction comes from the Lord and _condemnation_ comes from Satan. Conviction is very specific but condemnation is usually ambiguous. I found the following description to be very helpful:

> _"When He [Holy Spirit] is convicting you, pay attention! Be aware of what the Spirit of the Lord is trying to teach you. Be open to receiving His correction and what He is showing you that you need_

57

*to repent of and change in your life. The word 'repent' means to turn around. When the Holy Spirit convicts us, we need to turn around, change the way we did something or the direction we are thinking of proceeding. As we grow in our walk with the Lord we will be able to more quickly identify when it is conviction from the Holy Spirit or condemnation from the enemy. **When we receive condemnation from the enemy, it is different. He wants us to stew on what we did wrong and let it build up inside us. He is hoping we will take on the emotions of guilt, regret, blame and shame.** He wants these emotions to plant a seed inside us; telling us that we are no good, that we will do it again and nobody is going to forgive us for our mistakes."[36]*

The Bible says, "God resists the proud, but gives grace to the humble."[37] Living a life of repentance requires humility. Memorize the above verse. Now, spend your time in prayer today asking God for a humble heart so that He will not resist you and so that you will not resist Him. Pray for those you love that they too would be humble and willing to do whatever it takes to live close to God.

_____

[36] DeGraw, Kathy, "Discerning the Difference Between Holy Spirit Conviction and Demonic Condemnation," Charisma News, http://www.charismanews.com/opinion/49346-discerning-the-difference-between-holy-spirit-conviction-and-demonic-condemnation (accessed June 12, 2015).
[37] James 4:6 NKJV

WEEK

16

WHO IS
THE HOLY SPIRIT?

The Holy Spirit is *God*.

 GENESIS 1:26-27

Did you notice that in verse 26, when God speaks, He refers to Himself as "Us?" Christianity is a monotheistic religion (one God), so why does God use a plural pronoun?

The Bible teaches that God is a *trinity* (though the specific word is never used in the Bible).[38] Christians believe that there is one God and that He, having one nature (love), exists in three persons (Father, Son, and the Spirit). In other words, God is *one* and God is *three*. This is a paradox. A paradox is "something that is made up of two opposite things and that seems impossible

---

[38] The word 'trinity' is never used in the Bible though the concept is all throughout. This doctrine was formally confirmed and accepted as orthodoxy among early church leaders at the Council of Nicea in 325 A.D.

but is actually true or possible."[39] Only by faith can you grasp such truths.[40]

So who has the Holy Spirit?

 ROMANS 8:9 and ACTS 2:32-29

Only Christians have the Holy Spirit. If you do not have the Holy Spirit, you do not belong to Christ. At conversion, the moment you decided to put your faith in Jesus Christ, the Holy Spirit came to live inside of you.

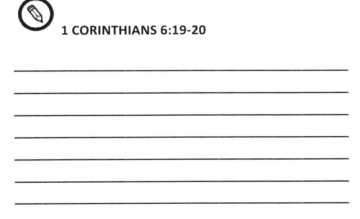 **1 CORINTHIANS 6:19-20**

_____

_____

_____

_____

_____

_____

_____

The Holy Spirit, the third person of the Trinity, actually makes His home inside of you now. Your spirit has been joined to Him.[41] As Paul wrote, you are now a "jar of

---

[39] "Paradox," Merriam-Webster.com, http://www.merriam-webster.com/dictionary/paradox (accessed June 9, 2015).

[40] I have Bruce Campbell to thank for helping me understand the importance of paradox in the Christian faith.

[41] 1 Corinthians 6:17 NKJV

clay" intended to host the "treasure" of the Holy Spirit.[42]

 JOHN 16:7-11

How could Jesus leaving be to our advantage? At first glance, this seems to be a rather ridiculous claim. But consider this: When Jesus was on earth, He was restricted by his physical body to being in one place at one time. If He was here, He could not be there. Or if He was there, He could not be here. You get the idea. The reason Jesus said that it was going to be *good* for Him to depart from the earth is because the Holy Spirit, who can be everywhere at once, would have the ability to be with multiple people simultaneously. Let this truth comfort you. You cannot sleep, eat, do homework, change a diaper, watch a movie, or go to work apart from God. He is in you! He will never leave you or forsake you. You belong to God, and giving you the Holy Spirit was His way of *sealing* the deal!

There is no other religion where God comes to actually dwell inside you. The Bible says that God the Father and God the Son (Jesus) are in Heaven. Only the Holy Spirit is here on the earth and the place He dwells is inside believers. Take some time right now to talk specifically to the Holy Spirit. You need to be comfortable interacting with Him. He is the one *always* with you because He dwells within you.

---

[42] 2 Corinthians 4:7

17

THE ROLES OF
THE HOLY SPIRIT

A gift is something that is given out of the kindness of someone's heart.

 ACTS 2:38

You read this verse yesterday. The Holy Spirit is depicted as a *gift.* He is given by God the Father[43] to His sons and daughters to them love, follow, become, and share Jesus Christ.

 JOHN 14:15-18, 14:25-26, 15:26

Jesus refers to the Holy Spirit as *Advocate* (*Helper* in some translations) in all three passages. He refers to the Holy Spirit as the *Spirit of Truth* twice. The word "advocate" in the original Greek language is the transliterated word **paracletos**, meaning "one called alongside to help; or Comforter, Advocate, Intercessor."

In my early 20's, I travelled across China. On this particular occasion, I was taking a 24-hour train ride across the desert in West China. The mission group I

---

[43] John 14:16, 14:26, and 15:26 clearly state that the Father is the One who gives the Holy Spirit.

was co-leading had paired up with a long-term missionary and was going to share the Gospel of Jesus Christ among the *Tajiks*. On the train, the long-term missionary and I got into a conversation with two men from China. After the long-term missionary shared about Christ, the two men began to converse back and forth. I asked her what they were saying. She told me that one man was attempting to summarize to his friend what we had just shared. He told his friend that the God of Christians was the God who came to earth so he could put His arm around us and help us. Wow. This was the description of a man who did not yet profess Christ. What truth!

In John 14:15, we are told that if we love God, we will obey. In the very next verse, Jesus teaches that God is going to send another Helper. You must read this in context. Jesus was saying that though God expects His children to obey, He at the same time is coming in the form of the Spirit to live inside of His people and once there, will be in position to help each Christian obey. He does not give a command from a distance and then leave you to yourself. By living inside of you, He is able to strengthen and empower you to actually do what He has commanded. No other moral philosophy (Aristotle's *Virtue Ethics*, John Stuart Mill's *Utilitarianism*, Kant's *Deontological Ethics*, etc.) or religion offers such a Helper. Christianity is unique in that the same God who commands also bends low to give us the powerful assistance we need to obey those commands. He is a good God. He is for us, not against us.[44]

---

[44] Romans 8:31 NKJV

Secondly, at the end of verse 17, we are told that the Holy Spirit will live with us and be in us. Then, in verse 18, Jesus immediately says that He will not leave us orphans. Connect the dots. One of the main jobs of the Holy Spirit is to convince you once-and-for-all that God is now you're Dad and that He is for you, not against you.[45]

 ROMANS 8:14-17

The Holy Spirit is also referred to as the *Spirit of Truth.* He will speak, lead, guide, and help you every step of the way. This *truth* may be a word of encouragement from the Father's heart or it may be in the form of *conviction.* Either way, Daddy has your good at heart. You can trust Him.

Prayerfully meditate on the truth that the Holy Spirit's main job is to come alongside you and help in all areas of your life. Reflect upon the goodness of the Lord to send such a Helper. Now, invite the Holy Spirit to help you one area at a time. Where do you need it most?

_____

_____
_____
_____

---

[45] Romans 8:31

18

THE FRUITS OF
THE HOLY SPIRIT

How can a person claim to be a Christian and yet remain unchanged? After all, you have the Holy Spirit living inside of you.

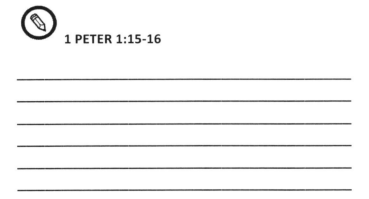 **1 PETER 1:15-16**

_____

_____

_____

_____

_____

_____

God commands every believer to be holy. To be *holy* means to be *set apart.* This is a two-sided coin. A Christian is to be set apart *from* the world while being set apart *unto* God.[46] But what does it mean to be set apart from the world? After all, did Jesus not say, ""My

---

[46] I first learned of this *from-to* distinction while listening to Todd Goodwin.

prayer is not that you take them out of the world but that you protect them from the evil one."[47] What gives?

The "world" stands for every *arrangement* (i.e., marital, ecclesiastical, moral, political, economic, etc.) that goes against who Christ is and what He has revealed to be true. As humans, we live, eat, sleep, talk, work, and play in this world. So obviously, God was not telling us to go live in space or forego our normal responsibilities. Rather, He was teaching that His people are to go about the business of their lives in a Christ-centered manner.

 1 THESSALONIANS 5:23-24

The process by which one becomes holy is called *sanctification.* Wayne Grudem writes, "Sanctification is a progressive work of God and man that makes us more and more free from sin and like Christ in our actual lives."[48] It is a partnership. God has a part to play and we do as well. His role is active. He is the only One who possesses the power to change you. Your role is passive. You must be available to Him, spend time with Him, and at all times answer "yes" to all that He wants to *actively* accomplish.

WRITE DOWN THE 9 FRUITS OF THE HOLY SPIRIT MENTIONED IN GALATIANS 5:22-23

---

[47] John 17:15

[48] Wayne Grudem, *Systematic Theology: An Introduction to Biblical Doctrine* (Grand Rapids: Zondervan, 1994), Kindle e-book.

Sell your books at
sellbackyourBook.com!
Go to sellbackyourBook.com
and get an instant price
quote. We even pay the
shipping - see what your old
books are worth today!

Inspected By: karolina_gamez

00067611729

1. _____

2. _____

3. _____

4. _____

5. _____

6. _____

7. _____

8. _____

9. _____

This is a list of what the Holy Spirit, over time, desires to grow in the soil of your heart and character. Your *flesh*, the sinful part of your nature that is in opposition to God, must yield. Before Christ, you did not have any power to overcome your carnal (another name for flesh) nature. But now, with the Holy Spirit inside of you, there is a greater power at your disposal enabling you to live as a "slave of righteousness" rather than a "slave to sin."[49] Essentially, this list is first and foremost a description of God's nature. **As the Holy Spirit cultivates these fruits[50] in your heart and life, you will become holy, less like the world and more like Christ.** The Holy Spirit will sanctify you, making you more like Christ, and thereby setting you apart for Himself and His service.

---

[49] Romans 6:17-19 NASB
[50] Psychologically speaking, *character traits*

Paul writes that as Christians, we are continually to be "growing in the knowledge of God."[51] Take a few moments, one fruit at a time, and meditate on how each fruit listed is first and foremost a character trait of God. God is love. God is joy. You get the idea.

_____

_____

_____

_____

[51] Colossians 1:10

19

THE GIFTS OF
THE HOLY SPIRIT

A gift, just like salvation and the Holy Spirit, is to be received and *opened* with thankfulness. So many churches today are dead, empty, and boring because they are not open to the Holy Spirit or His gifts.

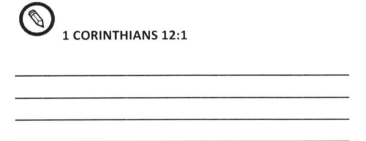

1 CORINTHIANS 12:1

_____

_____

_____

_____

This is a strong word. He commands each follower of Christ to not be ignorant (uninformed, unaware) of spiritual gifts. This involves not just knowing the list of gifts, but more importantly, the gifts He has deposited in you. What are the gifts?

 **1 CORINTHIANS 12:8-10, 12:28, EPHESIANS 4:11, and ROMANS 12:6-8**

Christians disagree on the exact number of spiritual gifts. That being said, their disagreement is minor.

Below is a list of the gifts you just read (some are repeated and therefore not mentioned twice in the list).

- Word of wisdom
- Word of knowledge
- Faith
- Gifts of healing
- Miracles
- Prophecy
- Distinguishing between spirits
- Tongues
- Interpretation of tongues
- Apostleship
- Teaching
- Helps
- Administration
- Evangelism
- Pastoring
- Serving
- Encouraging
- Giving
- Leadership
- Mercy

So what does God want you to do with this list?

First of all, *pray*. God responds to a hungry, inquisitive heart. Why would He give you a gift/s and not want to tell you? Make the simple choice to trust in His good heart. A good dad loves to speak to His children.

Secondly, be patient as you wait for revelation. Paul wrote, "All [gifts] are the work of one and the same Spirit, and He distributes them to each one, just as he determines."[52] This same Spirit who has given you gifts also lives inside of you. Quite often, discovering your gift-set is a process and therefore, takes time. Cry out to the Lord for revelation, but do not be anxious. He will pull back the curtain when He is ready.

Third, ask the people in your faith community who have been walking with Christ longer than you. A pastor, mentor, teacher, small group member, or friend may prove to be a great asset in your discovery process. Sometimes it is easier for someone else to see something God has placed in you than it is for you to see it yourself.

Lastly, start serving in your local church. Do not wait until you discover your particular set of spiritual gifts. Many times God will give insight as you go about *His* business. As you serve in your local faith community, He will orchestrate situations, conversations, and happenings that will eventually result in clarity.

 1 CORINTHIANS 12:7

_____

_____

_____

You are to use every spiritual gift you have been given to serve, encourage, and build others up. Your church should be better because you are using your gifts to

---

[52] 1 Corinthians 12:11

serve others rather than using your gifts to promote yourself. Serve like Jesus with all you have been given.

When you read the list of spiritual gifts, did any of them stand out? Talk to God. Begin today inviting the Holy Spirit to pull back the curtain in order to show you your unique gift-set. Decide now that you will not waste *His* gifts. Also, ask the Lord to help you recognize and appreciate the spiritual gifts He has placed in others. Pray for a *cooperative* rather than a *competitive* heart.

_____

_____

_____

_____

20

FILLED WITH THE HOLY SPIRIT

The Holy Spirit is our friend, helper, and teacher. He is a great gift from Daddy God to help each believer know God, love God, obey God, and become more like Christ His Son. You are never alone.

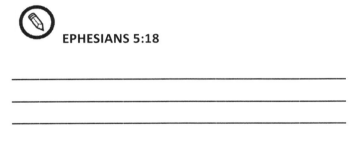 **EPHESIANS 5:18**

_____

_____

_____

_____

Paul instructs Christians to be "filled" with the Holy Spirit. This suggests that you can have the Holy Spirit yet not be full of Him. As Pastor Allen Hickman phrases it, "We leak." It is not that you literally have less of the Holy Spirit. What I believe Paul is teaching is that as we go about our daily lives, it is easy to put God on the backburner. When we do this, over time the person and work of the Holy Spirit is diminished and the both of you grow out of sync.

 JOHN 20:19-22

This story takes place after Jesus had died on the cross and was raised from the dead. He appears to His disciples. After blessing them with peace, He says, "Receive the Holy Spirit." At this moment the disciples received the Holy Spirit just as you did when you repented and turned to Jesus Christ.

 ACTS 1:1-8

Though the disciples had already received the Holy Spirit, Jesus promised them that the Holy Spirit was going to come and baptize them and that as a result, they would have great power and boldness to His witnesses.

 ACTS 2:1-4

Jesus' promise was fulfilled on the Day of Pentecost, a special day in the Jewish community. This is officially when the church began. At this moment, the disciples were "filled with the Holy Spirit."[53]

 ACTS 4:8, 31

In verse 8, the Bible says that Peter was full of the Holy Spirit. But then, in verse 31, we read that as Peter and the other believers gathered prayed, they were once again "filled with the Holy Spirit." So Peter, who was full of the Holy Spirit, was now being filled again with the Holy Spirit.

---

[53] Acts 2:4

God wants to constantly fill, refill, and fill again. We need it. Wayne Grudem puts it best when He writes, "Therefore, it is appropriate to understand the filling of the Holy Spirit *not* as a *one-time event* but as an *event that can occur over and over again in a Christian's life.*" He goes on to write,

> *"A balloon...can be 'full' of air even though it has very little air in it. When more air is blown in, the balloon expands and in a sense it is 'more full.' So it is with us: we can be filled with the Holy Spirit and at the same time be able to receive much more of the Holy Spirit as well."*[54]

As you read in verse 31, the fresh filling of the Holy Spirit released more boldness in their lives to step out and do God's will. Too many Christians have settled for a faith without much power. Churches have done the same. It is time that individuals and churches alike cry out for more and more of the Holy Spirit.

 Reflect on the balloon analogy. Now, cry out to God with all of your heart that He fill you with His Holy Spirit today more than ever before. Ask God to put a spiritual hunger/thirst in you for more of Him that will continue to grow throughout your entire life.

---

[54] Wayne Grudem, *Systematic Theology: An Introduction to Biblical Doctrine* (Grand Rapids: Zondervan, 1994), Kindle e-book.

WEEK

5

21

CHURCH:
THE HOPE OF THE WORLD

Bill Hybels writes, "The local church is the hope of the world."

While Jesus was on earth, He was a carpenter. He learned this trade from his father, Joseph. It was not until He was 30 years old that He began his focused ministry.[55] Throughout these three years, 12 men followed Him everywhere. The four Gospels (Matthew, Mark, Luke, and John) chronicle this time period. One of the more well-known conversations Jesus had with His disciples occurs in the following passage.

 MATTHEW 16:13-20

Peter responds to one of Jesus' questions with, "You are the Messiah, the Son of the living God." Jesus then tells Peter that He will build His church on this revelation.

What is the church? The transliteration of the Greek word for church is *ekklēsia.* It means "a calling out."[56] The church is a group of people who have been *called out* from the world to love, honor, and glorify Jesus Christ.

---

[55] Luke 3:23

[56] James Strong, *Strong's Hebrew and Greek Dictionaries*, e-Sword, Ver. 10.1.0, Dictionary, G1577.

Francis Chan writes,

> *"The church is a group of redeemed people that live and serve together in such a way that their lives and communities are transformed. God intends for every follower of Jesus to be a part of such a gathering under the servant leadership of pastors who shepherd the church for the glory of God."[57]*

Approximately 40 days after His resurrection, Jesus ascended into Heaven leaving the monumental task of spreading the good news to everyday, imperfect people.

 ACTS 2:42-47

From the very beginning, ordinary people have come together to eat, laugh, cry, pray, fast, worship, search the Word, and live life together. In the above passage, people were so in love with God that they were selling material possessions in order to provide for other Christians who were in need. The love of Christ had so captured their hearts that they were willing to sacrifice for one another.

Let God overwhelm your heart with His love for the church. The Bible describes the church as the bride of Christ. How can you love God but not care about the church? Spend some time in prayer asking the Holy Spirit to fill your heart with His love, wisdom, and

---

[57] Francis Chan, *Multiply* (Colorado Springs: David C Cook, 2012), 52-53.

perspective regarding the church (of which you are now a part of).

_____

_____

_____

_____

22

CHURCH:
BEING A PART

The word "church" can mean two different things. The *global church* is comprised of all Christians everywhere. If you are a Christian, you are part of the global church.

The *local church* is each particular body of believers all throughout the world. For example, Resurrection Life Worship Center is a local church. Grace Fellowship Ministries in Winnsboro, Texas is a local church. God desires, expects, and commands every disciple of Christ to be involved in a church community.

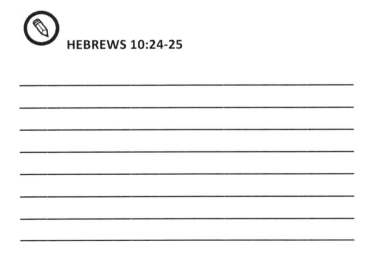

HEBREWS 10:24-25

_____

_____

_____

_____

_____

_____

_____

_____

God encourages us (it is actually a command) to "not [give] up meeting together."[58] In other words, you need other Christians and other Christians need you.

Attending a service once a week in a building does not mean that you are a "part" of the church. If you stand in your garage, do you become a car? If you crawl into a dog house, does this make you a dog?

In America's radically individualistic society, people do not want to depend on anyone. But this is *not* the way of Christ. You cannot sit in front of your television on a Sunday morning, listen to a preacher, make a donation online, and count that as your "church." Being a part of a church requires you to rub shoulders with real people. You have to make the choice, sometimes a difficult one, to be vulnerable and to allow people into your space.

When I lived in Kansas City, I met a lady from Germany. One day she asked me, "Do you know what we Germans say of Americans?" After I told her that I did not, she went on to state "Americans are five miles wide and one inch deep."

We have hundreds, even thousands, of "friends" on Facebook. We are more connected than any other generation in Western history. However, this "connection" is deeply superficial. People are dying from loneliness, and sadly enough, this is even true for many Christians who attend a religious service each week surrounded by people who never become anything more than a casual acquaintance. You, not the preacher, have to choose whether or not you are going

---

[58] Hebrews 10:25

to go through religious motions on Sunday or truly obey God and be a genuine part of a local body.

 EPHESIANS 2:19-23, 4:11-32

Church is a greenhouse, a place where you will mature as you open up to people and people open up to you. This does not happen quickly. It takes time. This is the reason that people who hop from church to church never stand a chance to fulfill God's purpose in their life. They are never in one place long enough to put down roots. For the church to truly be the hope of the world, the people who make up the church must decide to go beyond shallow conversations and empty connections. God matures His people in the rich soil of friendship.

 Some people are scared to be honest and open with the people around them. However, if you are really going to *be* part of the church, there must be those in your local church family with whom you are vulnerable and transparent. If trusting people is difficult for you, begin today asking God for courage. Also, pray to your Father in Heaven that He would *go before you*[59] to prepare these friendships. You will need them.

---

[59] Psalms 16:8 NKJV

23

CHURCH:
PLAYING YOUR PART

There is a difference between *being* and *doing*. Yesterday was about *being* a part of the church. Today is about you stepping up to the plate and swinging the bat.

 EPHESIANS 2:10

_____
_____
_____
_____

You have a job to do. Every family member is expected to pitch in and serve. There comes a point in which merely receiving becomes sin.

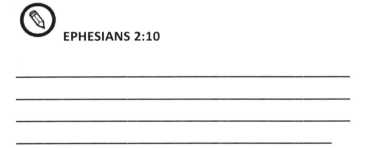 **1 CORINTHIANS 12:12-27**

Paul used the human body as a metaphor for the church. You may be an eye, someone else a toe, and another person an arm. Each part is designed by God to work in harmony with all of the other parts so that as a whole, the entire church (i.e. body) is strong.

Too often the church suffers because one member is jealous that someone else has a more up-front role. This person fails to recognize that "God has placed the parts in the body, every one of them, just as he wanted them to be."[60] Do not be selfish. Be willing to humble yourself and do what is needed. Consider asking your pastor if there is anything that needs to be done that no one else wants to do. Then make sure you follow through.

If you have a heart for kids, then get involved with children. If you enjoy interacting with youth, then volunteer to help with the teenagers. Maybe you enjoy making people smile. If this is the case, volunteer to greet people at the door when they enter. Maybe you are in a smaller church and the lead pastor wears 50 different hats during the week. Give him a call and commit to cleaning the church, mowing the grass, or cleaning toys in the nursery. Quit looking for a stage.

Bill Hybels writes,

> "A profound truth [is that] the church was designed to be primarily a volunteer organization. The power of the church truly is the power of everybody as men and women, young and old, offer their gifts to work out God's redemptive plan."[61]

In Christianity, the phrase "priesthood of the believer" means that in the New Testament age, every believer is a priest, one chosen to minister to people on God's behalf.

---

[60] 1 Corinthians 12:18

[61] Bill Hybels, *The Volunteer Revolution* (Grand Rapids: Zondervan, 2004), 31.

Some people open their hearts to people (what we discussed yesterday), but they will not serve. On the other end of the spectrum, others are willing to serve but never find the courage to open up and be transparent and real. You can serve every day of your life and still keep people at a distance. God wants you to take both steps. *Be* a part of the church and *play* your part in the church. Don't be a mooch.

In order to play your part, you may have to rearrange your schedule so that you can be a part of actively building God's church. Pray that God would reveal your *niche.* He has a specific place for you to serve in your local church family. See if He brings anything to mind. Be willing to obey. Pray that God give you a team-oriented heart. You need people and people need you.

_____
_____
_____
_____

24

CHURCH:
GIVING YOUR PART

One of the main metaphors in the New Testament for God's people is *family.* When you put your faith in Christ you became God's child. Therefore, every other person who has made this similar decision is now your *brother* or *sister* in Christ.

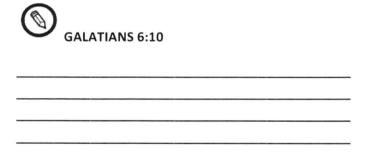

GALATIANS 6:10

_____

_____

_____

_____

We are a spiritual family, the household of faith. In a healthy family, each member is expected to contribute. It is no different in the church. Paul writes, "for each one should carry their own load."[62]

Though there are several ways to contribute to your local church family, I want to discuss one in particular—*money.* Whether we want to admit it or not, running a church requires money. Mortgage/rent, utilities, material for individual ministries, outreach events,

---

[62] Galatians 6:5

VBS's, children/youth camps, helping people in the body that need financial assistance, supporting missionaries, helping the poor, and staff salaries are only a few of the costs that arise in the life of a church.

So how much does God tell us to give to the church? In Old Testament times, God's people were commanded to *tithe*.

 LEVITICUS 27:30-32

Essentially, tithing is giving 10% of your income. A Jew would bring 10% of his produce/herd/flock to the priests at the temple. This supported the priests, the Old Covenant ministers. Many leaders, pastors, and churches teach that as Christians under the New Covenant, we too are commanded by God to give 10% to the local church of which we are a part.

The problem some Christians have with this conclusion is that tithing is barely mentioned in the New Testament. Jesus only mentioned tithing once, and when He did, it was regarding the Jewish temple, not the New Testament church.[63] And Paul, who wrote 13 of the 27 books in the New Testament, does not mention tithing even once and the majority of his books were letters instructing local churches how to conduct their affairs. Now, tithing is mentioned five times in the book of Hebrews,[64] but these references are merely historical in nature.

---

[63] Matthew 23:23; Luke 11:42
[64] Hebrews 7:5-9

So what does the New Testament teach about giving to the church and by extension, ministers?

 LUKE 10:27 and 1 CORINTHIANS 9:13-14

For preachers to be supported, members of a church must give. Jesus affirms that those called to preach the Gospel are to be supported by the people so they can devote themselves fully to the work.

 2 CORINTHIANS 8:1-4

The members of the Macedonian churches gave "beyond their ability" and "of their own accord."[65] This seems to imply much more than 10%. They were willing to sacrifice financially because they cared about the spreading of the Gospel, the health of the church, and the care of its leaders.

As I stated earlier, there are different views regarding tithing. Whether you believe in giving a flat 10% or not, what *is* clear is that all Christians are called to contribute financially in a significant, sacrificial way to the life and mission of one's local church family. Michael Morrison expresses this truth beautifully when he writes,

> *"People who entrust their lives to Jesus Christ do not worry about whether tithing is commanded in the New Testament. People who are being transformed by Christ to be more like Christ are generous. They*

---

[65] 2 Corinthians 8:3 NASB

want to give as much as possible to support the gospel and to support the poor."[66]

So what are we to conclude from all of this? Every Christian, including you, is called to give in a significant manner to the local church family of which you are a part. This is referred to as "storehouse giving."

 MALACHI 3:6-12

The Lord expects you to contribute financially to the life and mission of your church family. Give! Give! Give!

Imagine yourself walking up to God and putting all that you have (money and material possessions) in God's hands. Take some time to really surrender your "stuff" to Him. Hold everything with loose hands. Ask God to put in you a heart that loves to give to His church. Talk to Him about how much He wants you to give. Then obey immediately.

_____

_____

_____

_____

---

[66] Morrison, Michael, "Is Tithing Required in the New Covenant," Grace Communion International, https://www.gci.org/law/tithing (accessed June 27, 2015).

25

CHURCH:
THE ONE ANOTHER'S

A lawyer once asked Jesus, "Teacher, which is the greatest commandment in the Law?"[67] He replied,

 MATTHEW 22:37-40

Jesus had a way of simplifying things. He emphasized that every moral command in the Old Testament falls under one of these two commands—*loving God or loving people.* In the New Testament, one phrase that occurs almost 60 times is "one another." God's heart is for every Christian to live out their faith in a real, honest, transformational way with others who are also love Christ and want to know Him.

Look up the following verses. When you do, write the "one another" that is found in that verse (you do not have to write the entire verse).

JOHN 13:14 _____

_____

ROMANS 15:7 _____

_____

---

[67] Matthew 22:35-36

1 COR. 12:25[68] _____

_____

GALATIANS 5:13 _____

_____

GALATIANS 6:2 _____

_____

EPHESIANS 4:2 _____

_____

EPHESIANS 4:32 _____

_____

_____

COLOSSIANS 3:13 _____

_____

HEBREWS 3:13 _____

_____

HEBREWS 10:24 _____

_____

JAMES 5:16 _____

---

[68] "Cor" is short for Corinthians

1 PETER 4:10

_____

_____

_____

This is only part of the list. Francis Chan writes, "While every individual needs to obey Jesus's call to follow, we cannot follow Jesus as individuals. It's impossible to 'one another' yourself."[69] The _one another's_ of Scripture reveal that God's measuring stick for how much you love Him is how you treat other people in the household of faith. John wrote, "Whoever claims to love God yet hates his brother or sister is a liar. For whoever does not love their brother or sister, whom they have seen, cannot love God, whom they have not seen."[70]

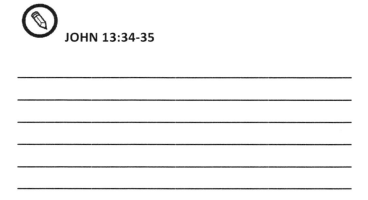

JOHN 13:34-35

_____

_____

_____

_____

_____

_____

The ultimate apologetic (i.e. a defense of the reality and goodness of God) is a body of believers loving one

---

[69] Francis Chan, _Multiply_ (Colorado Springs: David C Cook, 2012), 51.
[70] 1 John 4:20

another in a personal, sacrificial manner. Love is of the utmost importance because everything hinges upon it.

Do you remember the fruits of the Holy Spirit? The first one mentioned is "love." He produces love for God, love for yourself, and love for others in you. *He* does it. Take some time right now to ask God that by the work of His Spirit that you would be "rooted and grounded in love."[71] Do not get in a hurry. Wait on the Lord.

_____

_____
_____
_____

---

[71] Ephesians 3:17 NKJV

WEEK

6

26

EXTRAVAGANT GIVING

Jesus left Heaven, took on human form, and *gave* His life on the cross.

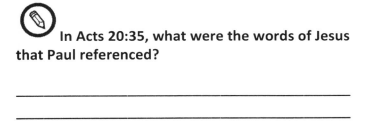 **In Acts 20:35, what were the words of Jesus that Paul referenced?**

_____

_____

_____

Extravagant giving lies at the heart of what it means to be a Christian. You may be thinking, "Did we not already discuss giving on day 24?" We did, but it was a very specific type of giving—*giving money to the local church you are a part of.* Becoming an extravagant giver is a much broader subject. More than something you do, giving is a lifestyle. To be a Christian is to be a giver.

 2 CORINTHIANS 9:6-11

God loves a cheerful giver. Verse 8 and 11 reveals the secret of cheerful giving—*God is able to bless you abundantly.* He is your source. As God told Abraham, "I will bless you...and you will be a blessing."[72] In every situation that the Holy Spirit leads you to give, you are able to give freely because of the confidence that God "will also supply and increase your store of seed"[73] as you bless others.

 MARK 12:41-44

The little ol' widow gave more than anybody else according to Jesus. She gave extravagantly. She wanted her money to go toward something bigger than herself. Jesus took great delight in her simple act and God was pleased.

You may decide to limit the amount of times you eat out each month so that you can give toward saving children in extreme poverty (16,000 die every day from hunger-related causes;[74] how are we as Christians not morally responsible to respond?). Or maybe God speaks to you about giving toward rescuing children out of sex trafficking. God may tell you to give away a car although you may feel that you cannot afford to do so. Maybe your church is actually involved in helping the poor (not all are) and you want to give money to help. Sponsor a teenager in your church so he or she can go to youth camp. Rather than being skeptical and judgmental, roll your window down and give some money or food to the

---

[72] Genesis 12:2
[73] 2 Corinthians 9:10
[74] "Hunger Facts," Compassion International, http://www.compassion.com/poverty/hunger.htm (accessed July 2, 2015).

person holding a cardboard sign on the street corner. Who really cares what he does with the money? Give!

One more note: A life of extravagant giving is not restricted to money. For many of us, *time* is more precious than money. Maybe you are this person. You would much rather relinquish money than time. But Jesus will ask you to do both. Following Christ is not always convenient, and if it seems so, you are probably not really following Christ. Will you give time to serve in your local church? Will you walk across the street and help your widowed neighbor take her groceries inside? Will you take the boy fishing that doesn't have a dad? If you love art, the Holy Spirit may lead you to create a piece that will minister to someone in a special way. Giving can look 1,000 different ways. The point is that you are ready and willing at all times to give whatever Jesus calls upon you to give.

If you are going to love Jesus, then you are expected to allow the Holy Spirit to stretch you and mold you into an extravagant giver. Obey Him every time He tells you to give. You cannot walk with Christ and be selfish.

Talk to God about giving. Is it more difficult for you to let go of your money, time, or both? Whatever you believe has the potential to keep you from becoming an extravagant giver, talk to the Lord about it. Transfer what owns your heart into the Lord's hands so He can own your heart. Ask God to create in you a heart that loves giving more than receiving.

27

A BIBLICAL WORLDVIEW

G.K. Chesterton wrote,

> *"But there are some people, nevertheless—and I am one of them—who think that the most practical and important thing about a man is still his view of the universe."*

He is referring to a person's overall worldview—*the big picture.* A worldview is a "set of beliefs and assumptions that a person uses when interpreting the world around him."[75]

Every single person has a worldview, a set of beliefs in response to questions such as,

- Does God exist?[76]
- Were human beings created or did we evolve?[77]
- What/who are we as humans?[78]
- Are humans essentially good?
- Are there moral absolutes?[79]
- How is marriage to be defined?

---

[75] [75] Slick, Matt, "Worldview," Christian Apologetics and Research Ministry, https://carm.org/dictionary-worldview (accessed July 6, 2015).
[76] Ibid.
[77] Ibid.
[78] Ibid.
[79] Ibid.

- Why is there suffering in the world?[80]
- Is there such a thing as an immaterial soul?
- What happens to someone at death?

The way you answer such questions will shape your desires, lifestyle, spending, media preferences, morality, faith, and behavior.

✎ PROVERBS 23:7

_____

_____

_____

_____

Your web of beliefs determines everything about you. If you were to pray for a man named John who has cancer and he fully recovered by the next day, Christians would claim that God healed John because Christians believe not only that God exists, but that He is good, powerful, and willing to heal. On the other hand, a naturalist (one who believes that there is no reality beyond the physical universe) would say that nothing supernatural happened in John's case because there is nothing supernatural that exists (no God, soul, or spirit). All that exists is the natural, physical, material world. In this worldview, one cannot speak of healing. A naturalist, by definition, can only offer naturalistic explanations of any phenomenon. People with different worldviews will interpret the same _exact_ events in completely different ways.

---

[80] Ibid.

One of the major problems today is that Christians are picking and choosing their personal, financial, relational, marital, social, moral, and political beliefs without even considering what God's Word has to say. John Stonestreet writes,

> The Bible is first and foremost a **metanarrative**, a grand, sweeping story that claims to be the true story of anything and everything that has ever existed. It begins with the beginning of all things, and ends with the end of all things. We, and all people, live in this story somewhere between Genesis and Revelation.[81]

Reality is defined and described in the pages of Scripture. It is incumbent upon every Christian to first and foremost turn to the Scriptures in order to discover the truth with which to base belief. A serious part of being a Christian is having a Biblical worldview. If you don't, your faith will suffer and we as Christians will lose our distinctive voice. If you follow Christ, think like Christ. On at least four different occasions Jesus asked His disciples, "What do you think?"[82] He was constantly poking and prodding their thinking. Why? He wanted

---

[81] Stonestreet, John, "PERSPECTIVES: Biblical Worldview: What It Is, and What It Is Not," The Chuck Colson Center for Christian Worldview, https://www.colsoncenter.org/the-center/columns/call-response/14732-perspectives-biblical-worldview-what-it-is-and-what-it-is-not (accessed July 7, 2015).

[82] Matthew 17:25, 18:12, 21:28, and 22:42 NKJV. Jesus used the word "think" at other times, but I refer here to the occasions He asked the exact question, "What do you think?" And of course this is dependent on the translation I used for this inquiry.

His followers to think like Him. I believe that this is in part what He meant when He called for each person to love Him with the entire mind.[83]

Get still and ask the Holy Spirit to show you what areas in your thinking are not in line with the truth revealed in God's Word. Ask with a submissive heart. In other words, allow God to correct you. He only does it for your good.

_____

_____

_____

_____

---

[83] Matthew 22:37

28

THE HEART
OF A SERVANT

Billy Graham, one of the greatest evangelists of all time, wrote,

> *"When Muhammad Ali, the heavyweight boxing champion, came to visit us in Montreat, he couldn't get over the fact that we did not live in a mansion with liveried servants and a chauffeur. He was also surprised when I met him at the airport in my ten-year-old Oldsmobile."*[84]

Christians are a "special people."[85] We should stand out. Those who belong to the Kingdom of God should look different than those who are still governed by the principles of this world. In a world full of people wanting everyone to serve them, few attitudes stand out like that of servanthood. Someone who serves others out of pure love rather than selfish-ambition is a remarkable witness for Christ. After all, the best way to shine for Jesus is to exemplify those characteristics of Christ that are most at odds with one's surrounding culture.

 JOHN 13:1-17

---

[84] Billy Graham, *Just As I Am* (New York: HarperCollins, 1997), 687.
[85] 1 Peter 2:9 NKJV

The washing occurred on the night before Jesus died on the cross. John chapters 13-17 are a record of Jesus' last words and actions. If you knew that death was near, you would say and do that which you deemed most important. Assuming Jesus had this same mentality, it is not insignificant that He among all things chose to model the *heart of a servant* before dying. When finished, Jesus looked at His disciples and said, "For I have given you an example, that you should do as I have done to you."[86]

MARK 10:43-45

_____

_____

_____

_____

_____

_____

_____

_____

_____

_____

If anybody deserves to be served, it is God. Yet, even Christ said that He did not come to be served, but to serve.

---

[86] John 13:15 NKJV

Will you demand that others serve you? Are you willing to love, pray for, and serve people who do not agree with you? Will you only serve those who respect you? When you serve someone, does the whole world have to know in order for you to feel it was worth it? Will you change churches because someone doesn't give you the attention or praise you deserve? All of these questions are related, for better or worse, to servanthood.

Yesterday one of my best friends called me. He had noticed that one of my car headlights was out. He asked what make and model my car was, bought the right lamp, and said he was coming over to fix it. Little did he know that I was home from work sick that day and that this "small" act of service would be a great blessing to me. Here are a few serving ideas:

- Bake cookies for your neighbors to bless them.
- Mow a widow's yard.
- Buy somebody a Bible or book that you think might minister to them.
- Write a personal letter or make a phone call.
- Wash someone's car.
- Pray for an individual. What better way to serve than to call upon God to help someone!
- Make coffee for your spouse.
- Serve your co-workers. Put them first. God can promote you. You do not have to step on others to get ahead.
- Commit to serving faithfully in your local church.

Tap into your likes, talents, hobbies, and spiritual gifts to serve people in creative ways. You never know which small act will bring someone into God's Kingdom!

Pray that God would place in you His servant's heart. What motives have driven you in the past? Were they selfish? James wrote that "selfish-ambition" is "demonic."[87] Hand every selfish motive over to God one-by-one and invite Him to purify your heart. When you have finished, take some time to ask God for a specific idea of how you can serve someone in a unique way today. If you are married, start there!

_____

_____

_____

_____

---

[87] James 3:14-15

29

GO! MAKE DISCIPLES

As a Christian, you are called to be a disciple of Jesus in every area of your life.

 LUKE 14:25-34

God is not telling Christians to literally hate their family members. So what is He saying? Nothing should interfere with loving, serving, and following Jesus Christ no matter the cost. However, there is more to being a Christian than being a disciple of Christ.

Jesus not only invites you to follow Him, but He also commands every Christian to disciple other people. You are to take what He has taught you and pass that on to others.

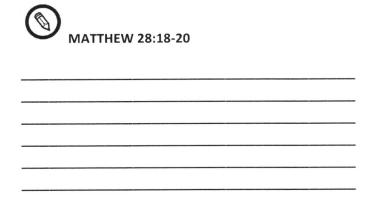 **MATTHEW 28:18-20**

_____

_____

_____

_____

_____

_____

_____

_____

This is one of the most famous passages in the Bible, known as *The Great Commission*. This commission is also recorded in the Gospel of Mark and reads a bit differently.

 MARK 16:14-20

Jesus does not give Christians permission to sit around and get fat on spiritual blessings. The church was never meant to be a "Jesus Bless Me" club. We are to receive from God so that we then have something to give to others on His behalf.

Making disciples is simple. You invite people to walk alongside as you walk out your faith in front of them. When you go to visit someone in the hospital or go to mow someone's yard, ask the person God has put on your heart to go with you. Becoming like Christ is *caught* more than it is *taught.* If there is a teenager in your church that doesn't have a dad, then call him and see if he wants to go fishing. If you start pouring into his life, before long, you will become the person he turns to when asking questions about life, girls, and God.

Recently, a man that works offshore shared that when he is on the boat, he teaches a Bible study for any of the men who are interested. This is discipleship. Discipling others means making yourself available to people, seeing who responds, and then pouring into them. It is not complicated. There will be moments when you need to be direct with an individual that God has laid on your heart. In these instances, do not be afraid to ask the person if he or she would like to meet up once a week for prayer and Bible study. Or, you may choose a book by a Christian author and go through it together. The bottom line is that there is an infinite number of ways that you can disciple someone. tick.

As you disciple others, you will grow in your faith. As you give your life away to help others grow in Christ, a sense of accountability will rise in your heart. You will become more aware that no man is an island to himself and that if you walk away from Christ or settle with compromise in one particular area, the people looking to you as an example will see it. And when they see it, your poor choices will discourage or even defeat their faith.

That being said, you do not have to be perfect to begin discipling someone. Most of the time, there will be no need to tell someone that you want to disciple them. Just start doing it. Be normal and as you hang out with the individual, look for God-ordained moments to share God's love and wisdom. Most importantly, trust God to use you. **Keep in mind that only God has the power to change someone.** This truth possesses the ability more than any other truth to guard you from becoming a manipulative, pressuring, aggressive person that pushes people further from Christ rather than drawing them closer. Love, pray, and leave the "changing" to God.

Talk with God about you being the disciple He wants you to be. Next, ask God the simple question, "Who have you brought into my life during this season that You are wanting me to disciple?" Do not get in a hurry. See if He will speak a name into your heart. Then pray about how He wants you to go about discipling the person.

_____

_____

_____

_____

30

SHARING YOUR FAITH

People tend to think of missionaries as Christians who have travelled to a poor, foreign land to live and share the Gospel. This is true, but this is not the full truth. *Every* **Christian is a missionary because every Christian is called to tell other people about Jesus Christ**. Interestingly, when Jesus delivered the man who dwelt among the tombs from thousands of demons (thus the name, "Legion"), He then instructed him, "Go home to your own people and tell them how much the Lord has done for you."[88] The point is that whether you stay or go, you are called as a Christian to live as a missionary for Jesus.

 LUKE 19:1-10

Zacchaeus was a crooked man who in all of his moral filth was so desperate to meet Jesus Christ that he was willing to climb up a tree so that Jesus would notice him.

Jesus tells Zacchaeus to come down immediately and they both go to his house. As evidenced by Jesus' claim, "Today salvation has come to this house," Zacchaeus received Christ into his heart that day as his Savior and

---

[88] Mark 5:19

Lord. He immediately began to tell Jesus everything he was going to do in order to make things right with the people he had wronged. This was true repentance.

The story ends with a very powerful statement. After Zacchaeus has repented, Jesus says "For the Son of Man has come to seek and to save that which was lost."[89] Jesus came to save people from their sins. He desires every Christian to partner with Him in carrying out this mission. We are His hands and feet. One should always be on the alert, looking for ways to tell people about Jesus Christ.

MATTHEW 5:13-16

_____

_____

_____

_____

_____

_____

_____

_____

_____

Christians are to be the salt of Jesus to an otherwise flavorless world. Christians are to be the light of Jesus in an otherwise dark and hopeless world. We do not need more preachers. We need _real_ Christians, ones that

---

[89] Luke 19:10 NKJV

actually care about people not going to Hell (the eternal destination of all who reject Christ). How can you believe in Jesus and not share your faith with family, friends, strangers, and even enemies?

Sometimes, Jesus will lead you to ask someone directly, "Are you a Christian?" At other times, the Holy Spirit is going to tell you not to say anything, but to be a Christ-like example to the people you rub shoulders with on an everyday, ordinary basis.

One of the great ways you can share your faith is by telling stories. A narrative is powerful. You may be in conversation with someone when an opportunity presents itself for you to share a story of something Jesus has done in your life. What is important is that we are sensitive to the Holy Spirit because He is going to lead us in specific ways from one situation to the next.

At the ballpark, college, workplace, golf course, book club, dance studio, or fishing league, the best place to start sharing your faith is with the people you see on a regular basis. This is *relationship evangelism.* Granted, there are times God will lead you to share the Gospel of Jesus Christ with a complete stranger. This being said, you will be most effective sharing your faith when you have taken time (weeks, months, maybe even years) to invest in another person's life. In the story of Zaccheus, Jesus actually went to his house and ate with him. He was not afraid to open his heart and live life with sinners. When someone knows you care about them, he or she will be most willing to hear what you have to share.

Peter, John, and a group of Christians once prayed, "Enable Your servants to speak Your word with great boldness."[90] Spend some time praying this prayer to God. Ask that He make you bold (not belligerent) in being a witness for Christ so that the fear of men (i.e. what people think, possible rejection, persecution) does not keep you from sharing your faith.

_____

_____

_____

_____

---

[90] Acts 4:29

ABOUT THE AUTHOR

B.J. Condrey was born in Winnsboro, Texas. Married to Allison, they have a son named Ezra. His educational background consists of the following:

B.A. Psychology
University of Missouri-Kansas City

B.A. Philosophy
University of Missouri-Kansas City

M.A. Philosophy
University of Southern Mississippi

B.J. served as a staff pastor in various roles (youth, college, small group, hospital visitation) at Grace Fellowship in Winnsboro, Texas and then at Resurrection Life in Picayune, Mississippi. After serving on staff as a pastor in the local church for over ten years, he entered the mission field of philosophy. He has taught philosophy at Pearl River Community College, Spokane Falls Community College, Whitworth University, and Gonzaga University. He will begin working on his PhD in *Christian Ethics and Practical Theology* in September 2017 at the University of Edinburgh where he was recently awarded a scholarship.

121

He has three other books available on Amazon in Kindle format and paper format—*"Where Does God Go?"*, *"The Word as a Vehicle,"* and *"Heal Me or Kill Me."* In addition, you can follow his blog at www.savethechristians.org.

PLEASE TAKE A MOMENT

Leaving feedback for this book on Amazon helps immensely. As a self-published author, nothing helps more than readers like yourself leaving feedback. Please do so now if possible. Thanks!

RECOMMENDED APPS

"On more than 180 million devices around the world, people are reading, listening to, watching, and sharing the Bible using the #1 rated Bible App—completely free. Over 1,000 Bible versions, in hundreds of languages. Hundreds of Reading Plans, in over 40 languages. Add your own Verse Images, highlights, bookmarks, and public or private notes. Customize your reading experience. Access everything when you're connected, or download specific versions for offline use. The Bible App lets you explore the Bible with your closest friends. Share honest conversations about Scripture with a community of people you know and trust. Learn along with them as you see what they're discovering."[91]

"Glo is an interactive Bible that brings the text of Scripture to life through HD videos, high-res images, articles, 360-degree virtual tours, and much more. Glo for iPad includes 4 lenses: Bible, Atlas, Media and the new socially-enabled "Me" Lens!"[92]

---

[91] Word-for-word description in iTunes app store.
[92] Ibid.

"Powerful Bible study tools linked to every verse in an easy-to-use, personalized Bible reader! Dig deep into God's Word with over 30 Bible versions, audio Bibles, text and audio commentaries, Hebrew / Greek lexicon, concordances, dictionaries, advanced word searches, and more. Customize your reading experience with rich color themes, fonts, auto scrolling, and parallel version views. Personalize your study with highlighting, underlining, and note taking options – all with Cloud back up."[93]

"Accordance is a fast and powerful Bible study app that lets you read, search, and explore the Bible. Read the Bible and follow along with a commentary or your own study notes. Compare two Bible translations side by side that will scroll in sync with one another. Follow a Bible reading plan. Take notes and highlights that will sync with the desktop version of Accordance. Search Greek and Hebrew Bibles (samples included) by lemma, inflected form, or root."[94]

---

[93] Ibid.
[94] Ibid. (only a partial description)

RECOMMENDED READING

Bonhoeffer, Dietrich	*The Cost of Discipleship*
Chambers, Oswald	*My Utmost For His Highest*
Chan, Francis	*Multiply*
Eldridge, John	*Wild At Heart*
Foster, Richard	*Celebration of Discipline*
Goff, Bob	*Love Does*
Graham, Billy	*Just As I Am*
Hall, Dudley	*Grace Works*
Lord, Peter	*Hearing God*
Manning, Brennan	*The Ragamuffin Gospel*
Manning, Brennan	*Ruthless Trust*
Meyers, Joyce	*Battlefield of the Mind*
Miller, Donald	*Blue Like Jazz*
Lewis, C.S.	*Mere Christianity*
Lewis, C.S.	*The Chronicles of Narnia*
Piper, John	*Desiring God*
Schaeffer, Francis	*True Spirituality*
Tozer, A.W.	*The Knowledge of the Holy*

Made in the USA
Middletown, DE
12 August 2018